A VISIT TO
Vietnam

REVISED AND UPDATED

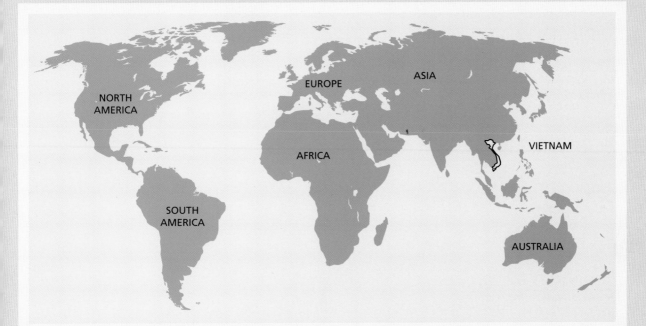

Peter and Connie Roop

Heinemann Library
Chicago, Illinois

Customer Service 888-454-2279
Visit our website at www.heinemannraintree.com

Designed by Joanna Hinton-Malivoire
Printed in China by South China Printing Company Limited

13 12 11 10
10 9 8 7 6 5 4 3 2

New edition ISBN-10: 1-4329-1276-3 (hardcover), 1-4329-1295-X (paperback)
New edition ISBN-13: 978-1-4329-1276-5 (hardcover), 978-1-4329-1295-6 (paperback)

The Library of Congress has cataloged the first edition as follows:
Roop, Peter
    Vietnam / by Peter and Connie Roop.
        p. cm. – (A visit to)
    Includes index.
    Summary: Describes many aspects of this long, narrow southeast Asian country including its land, landmarks, homes, food, clothes, schools, sports, celebrations, and arts.
    ISBN 1-57572-120-1 (library binding)
    1. Vietnam—Juvenile literature. [1. Vietnam.] I. Roop, Connie. II. Title. III. Series: Roop, Peter. Visit to.

DS556.3 .R66 2000
959.7—DC21
                                        97-37919

Acknowledgments
The publishers are grateful to the following for permission to reproduce copyright material:
© Getty Images p. **9** (Robert Harding World Imagery/Upperhall Ltd); © Hutchinson Library pp. **8** (C. Pemberton), **16** (R. Francis), **21** (S. Murray), **23**; © J. Allan Cash p. **28**; © Jupiter Images p. **17** (OnAsia/Chau Doan), **22** (Robert Harding/Tim Hall/Robert Harding); © Link Picture Library pp. **5** (K. Naylor), **6** (K. Naylor), **10** (K. Naylor), **12** (S. Kessler), **14** (K. Naylor), **15** (K. Naylor), **19** (K. Naylor), **20** (K. Naylor), **24** (K. Naylor), **27** (K. Naylor), **29** (S. Kessler); © Lonely Planet p. **13** (Oliver Strewe); © Robert Harding Picture Library pp. **11** (T. Waltham); © Still Pictures p. **25** (J. Schytte); © Trip pp. **7** (Vikander), **18** (A. Tovy), **26** (Viesti).

Cover photograph reproduced with permission of © Lonely Planet (Grant Dixon).

Every effort has been made to contact copyright holders of any material reproduced in this book. Any omissions will be rectified in subsequent printings if notice is given to the publisher.

Contents

Any words appearing in bold, **like this**, are explained in the Glossary.

Vietnam

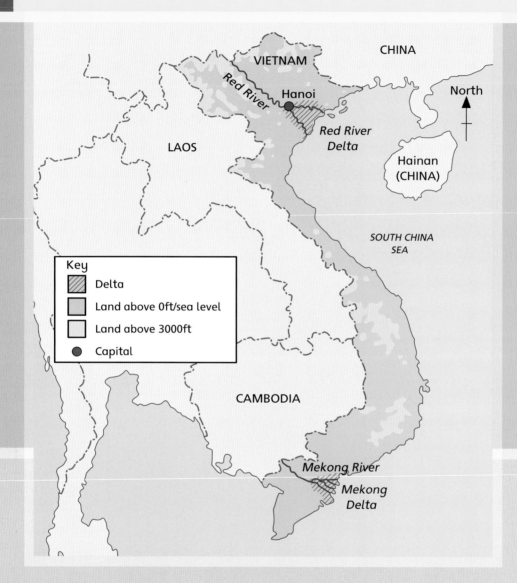

CHINA

VIETNAM

Red River

Hanoi

North

Red River Delta

Hainan (CHINA)

LAOS

SOUTH CHINA SEA

Key
- Delta
- Land above 0ft/sea level
- Land above 3000ft
- Capital

CAMBODIA

Mekong River

Mekong Delta

Vietnam is in southeast Asia. It is shaped like a giant letter S.

The people of Vietnam eat rice with most meals. Rice is grown in the lowlands in the middle of the country.

This Vietnamese woman has harvested her rice and taken the stalks off.

The west of Vietnam has many mountains. The east of Vietnam is next to the sea. There are rich, green lowlands in the middle.

Farmers plant rice in wet fields called rice paddies. Heavy rain floods the rice paddies in the **monsoon season**. The monsoons give good rice **crops**.

Water buffalo pull wooden **plows**.

Vietnam has two big rivers: the Red River and the Mekong River. Where they run into the sea, these rivers form **deltas**. Most people live in these deltas.

The streets of Hanoi are busy with all kinds of traffic.

Hanoi has been the **capital** of Vietnam for almost 1000 years. Long ago China ruled Vietnam. You can still see Chinese buildings in some places.

Most Vietnamese people live in small villages. Many homes are made of stone or **bamboo**. Few of these homes have running water or electricity.

City homes are small. Grandparents, parents, and children often share the same home.

Apartments in cities are very close together.

★ Food

People in Vietnam often eat food bought from food **stalls**. They eat their meals with **chopsticks** called *duon* (dwan).

People have their own bowl of rice and add the other food to it.

Meals are made up of lots of rice. It is put into a bowl with small pieces of vegetables, meat, or fish. *Nuoc cham* (nwahk chom) is a tasty sauce made from fish.

Clothes

Vietnam has a hot, **humid climate**. Most people wear loose, cool cotton clothes. Straw hats, called *non la* (non lah), help keep off the hot sun.

On special occasions, women wear an
ao-dai (aoh-doy). It is like a long shirt
and is worn with pants. Men wear *ao-the*
(aoh-theh) which is like a loose *ao-dai*.

Most Vietnamese people work in farming or fishing. Rice is the most important **crop**. Fruits and **sugarcane** also grow well in Vietnam's hot **climate**.

Workers in factories make clothes, glass, bicycles, bricks, and **electronic products**. People also **mine** coal. Coal is used for cooking or it is made into electricity.

Transportation

In the cities, most people travel on bikes, motorbikes, and cyclos. A cyclo is a three-wheeled bicycle. It is the Vietnamese taxi.

Children help look after the family's water buffalo.

Many people travel in boats on the rivers and **canals**. In the country they ride water buffalo. Water buffalo also pull carts and **plows**.

Languages

Most people speak Vietnamese. There are also groups of people who speak their own languages and have their own **traditions** and clothes.

The Vietnamese used to write *chu nom* (chew nom) which looked like Chinese. Now people write *quoc ngu* (kwok-new). It uses the English alphabet.

★ School

In Vietnam, all children go to school from the age of 6 to 11. They are in school six days a week. They learn many different subjects.

Students usually have to help their families bring in the **crops**. Most schools are closed at harvest time so they can do this.

Free Time

Most Vietnamese people work all day, for six days a week. When they relax, they play **pool**, soccer, and table tennis. They also like to swim and fish.

Sharing time with family and friends is important to the Vietnamese. They enjoy chess, cards, stories, and music with cups of hot tea or home-made sweets.

★ Celebrations

New Year, or Tet, can last for a week.
Everyone decorates their homes with
peach blossoms. Food, fireworks, and
games make Tet an exciting holiday.

People celebrate Trung Thu, the full moon festival, in August or September. Whole villages spend the day in dancing and singing.

The Arts

Vietnamese artists are famous for their jewelry, paintings on silk, and wood carvings.

Special water-puppet shows can only be seen in Vietnam. The puppets act out well-known stories, on lakes or ponds! People watch from the shore.

Name	The full name of Vietnam is the Socialist Republic of Vietnam.
Capital	The **capital** city is Hanoi.
Language	Most people speak Vietnamese but some can speak French or English, too.
Population	There are more than 85 million people living in Vietnam.
Money	Vietnamese money is called the dong.
Religions	Vietnamese people may follow Buddhism, Taoism, or Catholicism.
Products	Vietnam produces lots of rice, fish, oil, gas, and coal.

Words you can learn

chao (chow)	hello
tam beit (tahm bayeet)	goodbye
ban (bahn)	friend
cam on (cahm on)	thank you
da (dah)	yes
khong or khum	no
mot	one
hai (hi)	two
ba (bah)	three

Glossary

bamboo a tall plant with a long, strong stem

canal a river dug by people

capital the city where the government is based

chopsticks a pair of sticks held in one hand to lift food to the mouth

climate the normal type of weather for the area

crop plant that is grown for food

delta Sometimes a river slows down and leaves lots of mud as it enters the sea. This mud builds up and makes land called a delta.

electronic using electricity, like computers and televisions

festival party held by a whole town or country

humid when the air feels damp or wet

mine dig out of the earth

monsoon season a time of very rainy weather

plow the tool that farmers use to dig and turn over the soil before planting

pool a game played on a special table where each player has to hit the right balls into the side pockets

products things which are grown, taken from the earth, made by hand, or made in a factory

Southeast Asia the part of Asia that includes Cambodia, Laos, Burma, Thailand, Vietnam, Malaysia, and some other island countries such as the Philippines and Indonesia

stalls tables and shelves laid out with things for sale

sugarcane kind of tall grass that can be made into sugar

tradition way of doing things that has been done for a long time

★ Index